AVAILABLE NOW!

BE MORE GUS

CREATED BY EMILY BROOKS MILLAR

(ABOUT THE CREATOR)

EMILY BROOKS MILLAR IS AN AUTHOR & VISUAL ARTIST FROM SCOTLAND. SHE HAS ILLUSTRATED FOR BRANDS SUCH AS IMAGE COMICS, BBC & THE BIG ISSUE. HER PAINTING COLLECTIONS EXHIBIT INTERNATIONALLY AND CAN BE FOUND AT:

WWW.EMILYBROOKSMILLAR.COM

NATURAL SELECTION

(AS TOLD BY RATS)

REPRESS YOUR PAST

PLANT YOUR SEED

MAKE THEM BATTLE

DISOWN THE LOSER

PLANNING A PARTY

(AS TOLD BY RATS)

CURL INTO BALL

CHECK BELLY BUTTON STORAGE

CALL THE PHONE NUMBER

LET THE DRUG DEALER HOST

ADDICTION

(AS TOLD BY RATS)

HOW TO ORDER

(AS TOLD BY RATS)

BOOK THE BEST PLACE IN TOWN

WINK AT WAITRESS

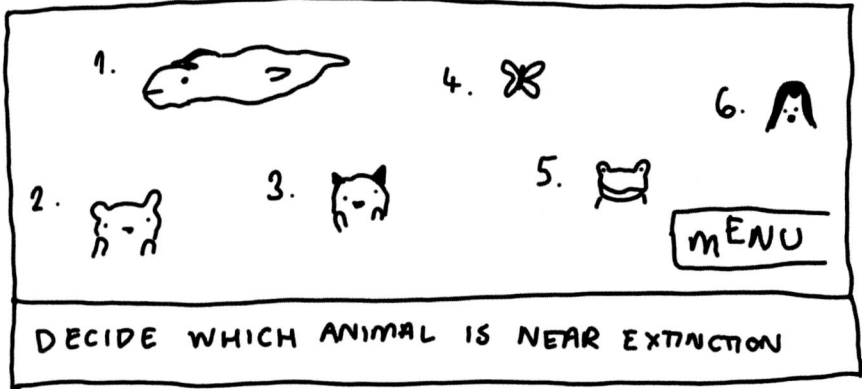

1.
2.
3.
4.
5.
6.

mENU

DECIDE WHICH ANIMAL IS NEAR EXTINCTION

ASSERT MASCULINITY

BECOMING A STAR

(AS TOLD BY RATS)

EMBARRASS YOURSELF

SEARCH ANONYMOUSLY FOR AN ANSWER

EVANGELICAL ADVICE

TERRORISE

GETTING A HAIRCUT

(AS TOLD BY RATS)

RULE #1: NO TALKING

RULE #2: HARD SLAPPING

RULE #3: FIRE

LEAVE ANGRY

AN AUTOBIOGRAPHY

(AS TOLD BY RATS)

HIRE A GHOST

ADD A SUDOKU

SKIM OVER TAX EVASION

FAKE CHARITY WORK

ACCEPT AN OBE

RAT CHAIR
(AS TOLD BY RATS)

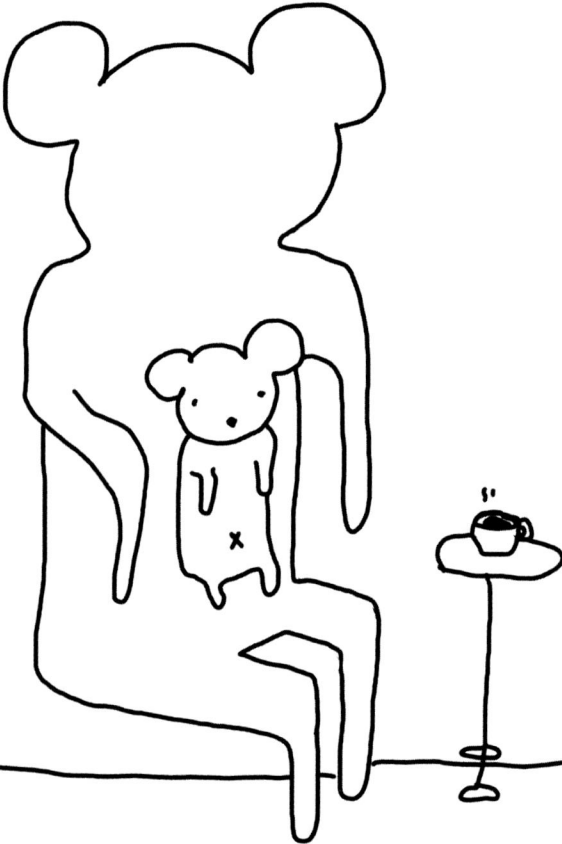

D R E A M S
(AS TOLD BY RATS)

FLYING A CARROT

FINDING OUT THAT YOU'RE JAMES BOND

SHOPPING NAKED

SEEING YOUR FAMILY DIE

PLAYING GUITAR

(AS TOLD BY RATS)

UNEMPLOYMENT

VISION BOARD

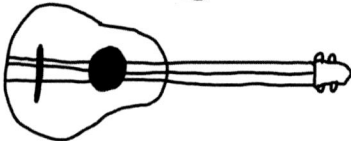

MANIFEST

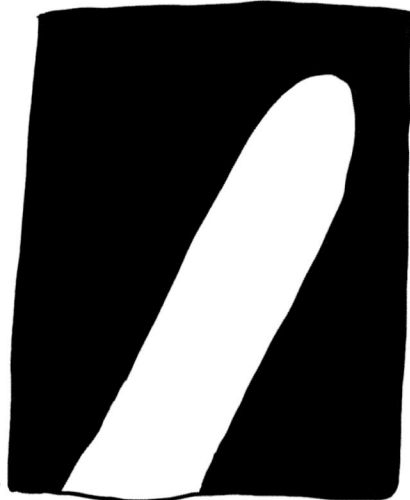

NO FINGERS?

TIME TRAVEL
(AS TOLD BY RATS)

ACQUIRE A PREPPY ENGLISH ACCENT

FIND NEAREST PORTAL

FIND A SIDEKICK

CALL HELEN KELLER A FRAUD

A TUBE JOURNEY

(AS TOLD BY RATS)

MAP

WAVE GOODBYE

"NEARLY" GET STABBED

EARPHONES WITH NO AUDIO

LEAVE WITH NEW DISEASES

MATERIALISATION

(AS TOLD BY RATS)

FRY TOFU

OIL BURNS

WATCH IT FORM

ADD BLOOD

A BABY IS MADE

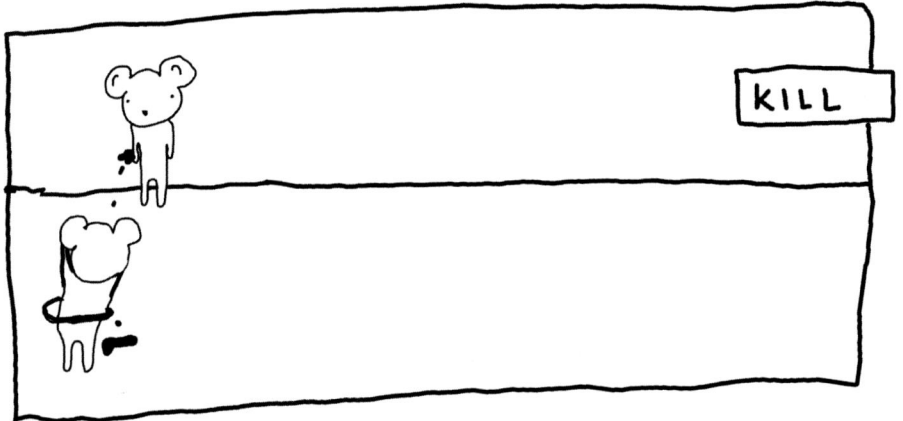

HOW TO STYLE A HAT

(AS TOLD BY RATS)

MAX OUT CREDIT CARD

TRY ON GRAPE

SHRIMP

ENEMY

PIN

CAPITALISE YOUR HOBBY

HOW TO SERVE
(AS TOLD BY RATS)

GROOMED BY
RECRUITER

SHOOT KIDS
FROM SKY

REPRESS

PRODUCE

(AS TOLD BY RATS)

DECIDE THAT DEATH IS YOUR VOCATION

RUN AWAY FROM OIL

GLOW AND THRIVE

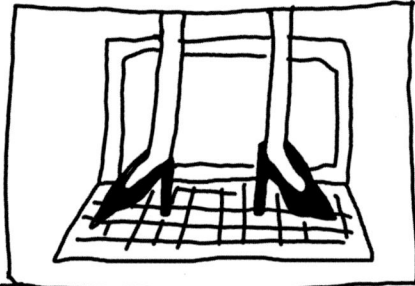

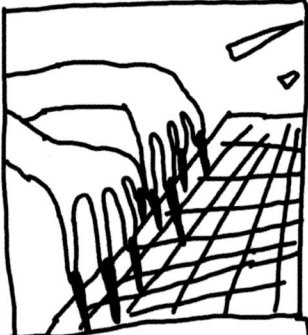

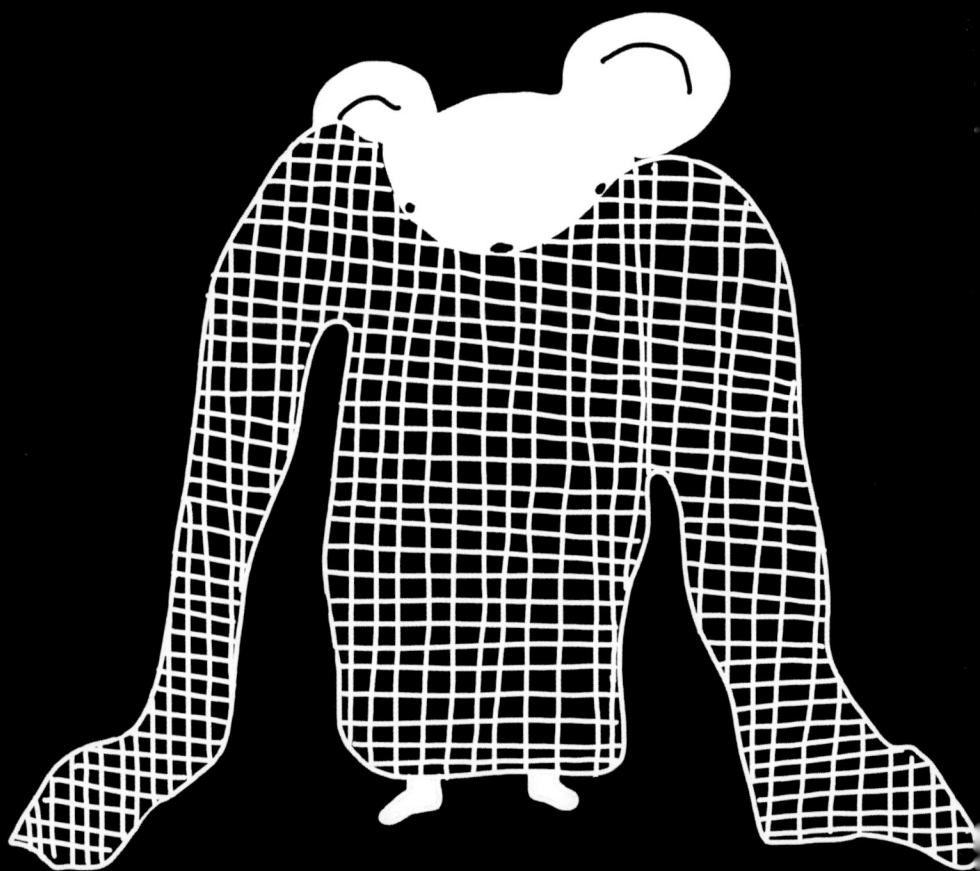

DONATING BLOOD

(AS TOLD BY RATS)

GOOD CITIZEN

RECEIVE COOKIE

USE RATS FROM YOUR BASEMENT

KIDNAP MORE

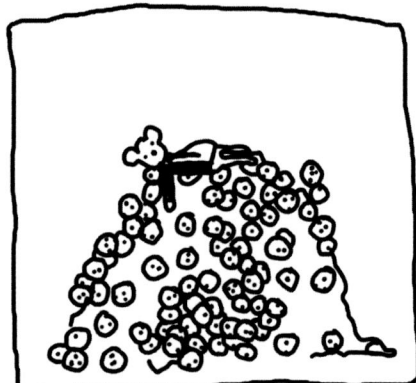

MANY COOKIES

CHRONIC ILLNESS

(AS TOLD BY RATS)

GET BITTEN BY A BUG

SUPER SKINNY

NO CURE

BECOME A SUPERMODEL

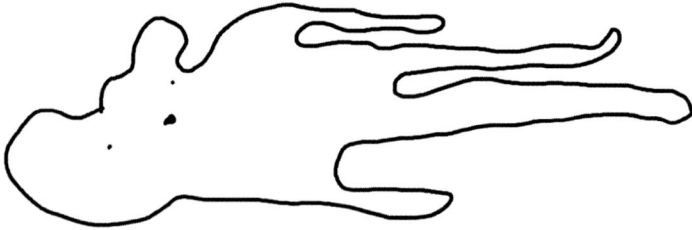

GOING TO THE DENTIST

(AS TOLD BY RATS)

PAIN

SCREAM

SUCK

FANGS

INDULDGE

(AS TOLD BY RATS)

AN EYE EXAMINATION

(AS TOLD BY RATS)

K
I LL
YOU
R FA
MILY

READ THE LETTERS

LOOK SUPER CUTE

RETURN HOME

USE EYESIGHT FOR GOOD

FINDING FRESH WATER

(AS TOLD BY RATS)

REALISE THAT YOU'RE GOING FERAL

EMBRACE

ASK YOUR **PARENTS** TO PAY FOR YOUR FLIGHT TO THE THIRD WORLD

FORGET WHY YOU'RE THERE

SHARE ONLINE

HOME INVASION

(AS TOLD BY RATS)

WATCH THEM SLEEP

SHARPEN BLADES

TIE UP KIDS

LEAVE WITH NICE LAMP

GOING TO A FUNERAL

(AS TOLD BY RATS)

PUT YOUR BEST JEANS ON

SEIZE THE OPPORTUNITY

DECLARE THAT YOU'RE A GHOST

SLEEP WITH HIS WIFE

SHOOT THE ZOMBIE

STRESS MANAGEMENT
(AS TOLD BY RATS)

RUNNING
(AS TOLD BY RATS)

BUY THE COSTUME

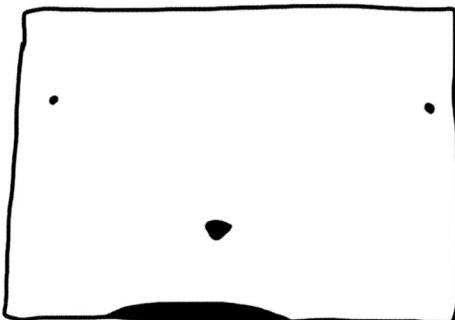

A S T H M A

RUN TOWARDS DANGER

KIDNAP THE KIDS

2022

(AS TOLD BY RATS)

ENJOY STRAWS

EAT DEAD STUFF

REJECT SCIENCE

FIND A FATHER FIGURE

AN ACT OF GOD OCCURS

A NEW IDENTITY

(AS TOLD BY RATS)

PURCHASE A BALACLAVA

CYBERSTALK THE RAT YOU WILL BE

TELL HIM HE'S A LOSER

😞	BAD RAT	👎
😐	SAD RAT	👎
😠	MAD RAT	👍

REPLACE HIM AT FAMILY DINNERS

HOW TO BOX

(AS TOLD BY RATS)

BECOME A STREAMER

INDOCTRINATE KIDS

BUY DESIGNER GLOVES

TAKE MONEY FROM BABIES

A BETRAYAL

(AS TOLD BY RATS)

WATCH FAVOURITE STREAMER

TEXT HIM FOR DAILY AFFIRMATIONS

TURN A BLIND EYE

GIVE CREDIT CARD INFO

WATCH HIM GET RAIDED

CANNIBALISM

(AS TOLD BY RATS)

MAXIMISE MARKET: GROW CHEAP & ORGANIC

PAY FOR ONLINE ADS

PAPRIKA

EMPTY STREETS

REAP THE BENEFITS

PERSUASION

(AS TOLD BY RATS)

USE FAME FOR GOOD

TEXT UNDERAGE RATS

EXIT

BECOME A FLIGHT RISK

RETALIATION

(AS TOLD BY RATS)

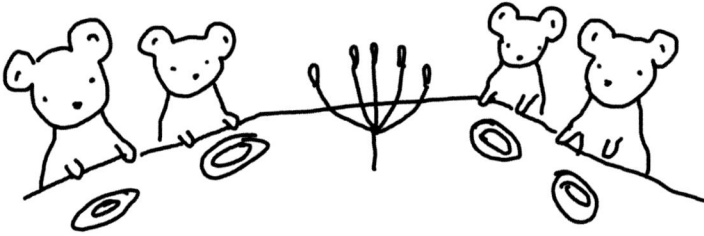

WATCH RAT BELITTLE YOU ALL NIGHT

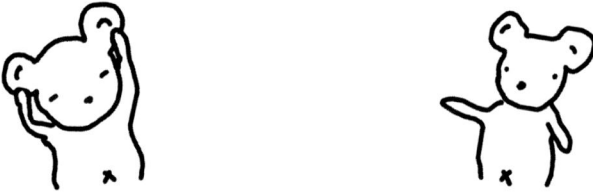

REALISE THAT HE CAN'T FEEL LOVE

BREAKIN NEWS

TANK HIS PYRAMID SCHEME

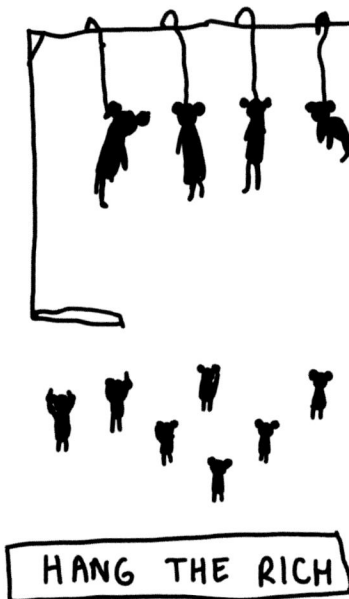

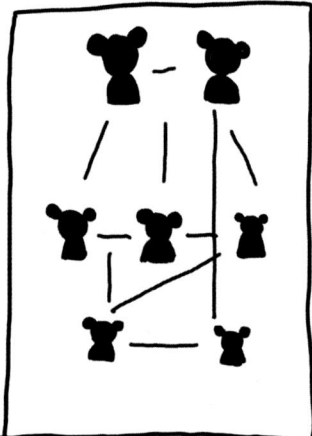

(AS TOLD BY RATS)

AS TOLD BY RATS LOOKS AT
THE SILLINESS, MORALITY AND
AUTHENTCITY OF FURRY
SOCIAL OUTCASTS.

—

THE LIFE LESSONS, DECISIONS
AND GENERAL ADVICE ENCLOSED
SHOULD BE TAKEN WITH A
PINCH OF CHEDDAR.

—

MANY RATS WERE HARMED
IN THE MAKING OF THIS BOOK.

A BROKEN APPLE

1

SUSPECT #01

MAKING A SHORT FILM

(AS TOLD BY RATS)

STEAL EXPENSIVE EQUIPMENT

CREATE A CASTING COUCH SITUATION

SECRETLY ADVERTISE VITAMINS

QUESTION WHO YOU ARE

PAY FOR YOUR VALIDATION

THE HUSTLE

(AS TOLD BY RATS)

LISTEN TO EVERYTHING
FROM CATHOLIC SCHOOL

BLEED FROM EYES

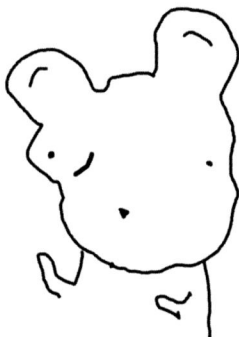

ANEURYSM

HOW TO FIND YOURSELF

(AS TOLD BY RATS)

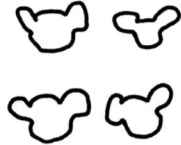

START A PODCAST

DECIDE WHICH TYPE OF RAT IS THE ENEMY

PROMOTE UNDERGROUND BUNKERS

ABSORB YOUR CO-HOST

APPLYING FOR JOBS

(AS TOLD BY RATS)

HAND OUT YOUR RESUME

REMEMBER IT'S NOT 2007

FIND RAT TO COPY

HEAR ABOUT HIS PASSING

HIS COLLEAGUES SUSPECT NOTHING

BECOME CEO

MANIFESTATION

(AS TOLD BY RATS)

DANCE AROUND YOUR ROCKS

IVERMECTIN INTO VEINS

LET POOR PEOPLE BUY YOUR MADE-UP CURRENCY

THANK GOD

DRIVING LESSONS

(AS TOLD BY RATS)

CRUSH YOUR TEACHER

ONLY DRIVE AT NIGHT

BUY SOME SERVICES

LANDLINES

(AS TOLD BY RATS)

QUESTION THE SCIENCE

FEEL THE GOVERNMENT CHEMICALS

SPEAK IN MORSE CODE

FIND A FAMILY IN YOUR WALLS

A PET

(AS TOLD BY RATS)

DO RESEARCH

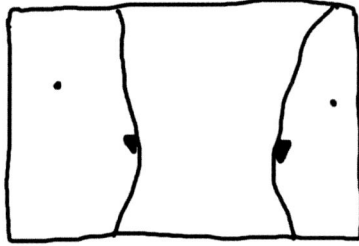

DISCUSS WITH PARTNER

PREPARE

EMERGE

KEEP ONE

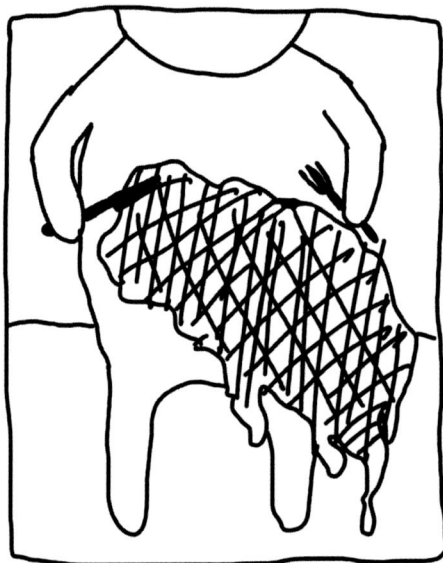

HOW TO MAKE SOUP

(AS TOLD BY RATS)

POTATO

CRY

SPICY TEARS

ORGANIC INGREDIENTS

CAST SPELL

POISON CHILD

A NEW JUMPER

(AS TOLD BY RATS)

SUCCESS AT THE THRIFT STORE

GET ATTENTION

THE PREVIOUS OWNER VISITS

TAKING OUT TRASH

(AS TOLD BY RATS)

S T A R E

BUNNY EARS

BUNNY IN THE HOLE

MAGIC TRICK

HEALING

(AS TOLD BY RATS)

SELL SELF IMPROVEMENT COURSES

HELP YOUTH

FIND A NEW STYLE

STAY HUMBLE

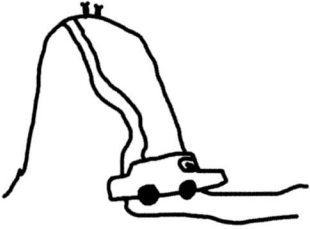

MARRIAGE

(AS TOLD BY RATS)

MEET THE LOVE OF YOUR LIFE

EXIST FOR THEIR PLEASURE

WATCH THEM LEAVE

GET JACKED

PROPOSE TO THE FIRST RAT YOU SEE

AFFECTION

(AS TOLD BY RATS)

PUT ON SPECIAL GLOVE

HEAD PATS

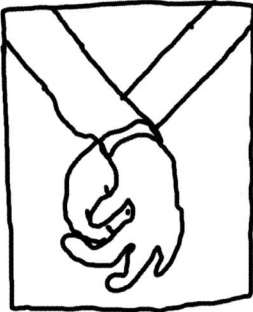

HAND HOLD

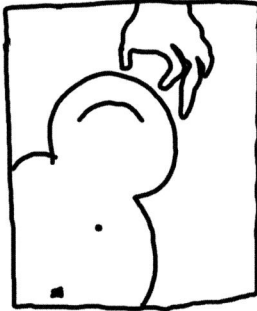

EAR HUG

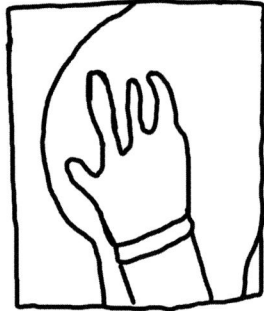

BUTT

NECK HUG

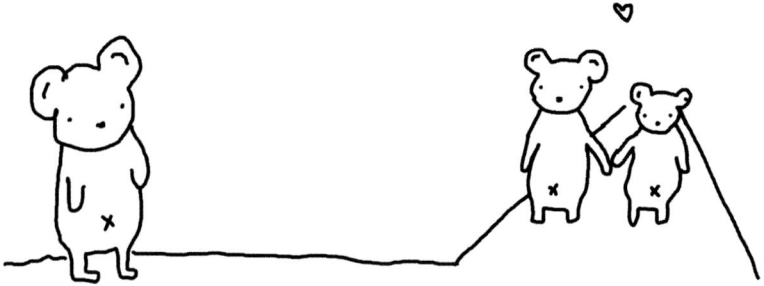

SHAKING HANDS
(AS TOLD BY RATS)

TICKLE

SNEAKY

WET

FOOT

ENGULF

DOUBLE TIME

HOLD

SLAP

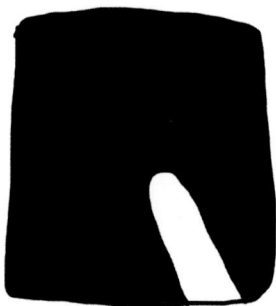

NICE TRY